W9-AKW-272

MY FIRST LOOK AT COUNTRIES

CANADA HAS SHORES BY THE OCEANS

Canada

ADELE RICHARDSON

CREATIVE EDUCATION

Published by Creative Education

123 South Broad Street, Mankato, Minnesota 56001

Creative Education is an imprint of The Creative Company

Designed by Rita Marshall

Photographs by Getty Images (Walter Bibikow, Wayne R. Bilenduke, Suzanne and

Nick Geary, Chung Sung-Jun, Paul Nicklen / National Geographic, Michael Orton,

Rischigitz, Philip & Karen Smith, Jennifer Thermes, Roy Toft / National Geographic,

Jacob Taposchaner, VCL)

Copyright © 2007 Creative Education

Printed in the United States of America

Library of Congress Cataloging-in-Publication Data

Richardson, Adele, 1966- Canada / by Adele Richardson.

p. cm. — (My first look at countries)

Includes bibliographical references.

ISBN-13 : 978-1-58341-444-6

1. Canada—Juvenile literature. I. Title.

F 1008.2.R525 2006   971 —dc22   2005050036

First edition 9 8 7 6 5 4 3 2 1

Canada

Big and Cold

Canada is a country on the **continent** called North America. It is at the top of the continent. Canada is close to the North Pole.

Canada is a big country. It is the second biggest country in the world! Only Russia is bigger.

GREENLAND

CANADA

UNITED STATES
OF AMERICA

MEXICO

Canada is next to the United States

It is very cold in the north part of Canada. North is the top part of Canada on a map. Winter can last for nine months there. Most lakes turn to ice during the winter. Summer is short and cool.

The south, or bottom, part of Canada is warmer. Winter only lasts about three months. Summer can get hot. Most people in Canada live in the south.

Between Canada and the
United States is a giant
waterfall called Niagara Falls.

The Land of Canada

Canada has many mountains. Some are very tall. They have ice on them all year long. Not many people live in the mountains.

Some of the land in Canada is flat. Few trees grow on the flat lands. The earth is used for farming. Farmers in Canada grow corn, beans, and wheat.

Canada's police are called
the Royal Canadian Mounted
Police or "Mounties."

MOUNTIES KEEP ALL PARTS OF CANADA SAFE

Some areas of Canada have lots of forests. The forests have many maple trees. There are lots of lakes in Canada, too.

Up north is the tundra. The ground of the tundra is frozen all year long. No trees grow there. In the summer, **moss** grows on rocks.

MAPLE LEAVES TURN COLORS IN THE FALL

WONDERFUL WILDLIFE

Many kinds of animals live in Canada. Moose and foxes make their homes there. Beavers live in the woods. Polar bears live in the cold north. They are the biggest bears in the world!

A lot of birds live in Canada, too. The snowy owl lives in the **Arctic**. Loons live all over the country. So do Canadian geese.

THERE ARE LOTS OF MOOSE IN CANADA

Some animals live in the cold ocean around Canada. Seals and walruses live there. So do whales. These animals have lots of fat. It helps keep them warm in the cold water.

PEOPLE OF CANADA

The first people to live in Canada were **Native Americans**. Many Native Americans still live in Canada. Some live in the cold Arctic. They are called the Inuit (*IN-yoo-it*). Some people call them Eskimos.

During the summer in the
north part of Canada, the sun
shines all day and all night.

CANADA HAS LOTS OF QUIET, PRETTY PLACES

People from France came to Canada about 500 years ago. People from England came, too. The people built houses. They explored Canada's land and rivers. Some **traded** with the Native Americans.

Today, some people in Canada speak English. Others speak French. Some people speak both languages. People from all over the world call Canada home!

PEOPLE FROM FRANCE EXPLORED CANADA'S RIVERS

HANDS-ON: CANADA'S FLAG

A maple leaf is on Canada's flag. You can use a leaf from any tree to draw Canada's flag.

WHAT YOU NEED

A piece of white paper

A red crayon

A leaf

WHAT YOU DO

1. Lay the paper so it is more wide than tall.
2. Lay the leaf in the middle, pointing up. Outline it with the crayon.
3. Turn the leaf so it makes an "L" with the leaf you just drew. Outline the leaf again.
4. Turn the leaf so it makes a backwards "L" with the first leaf. Outline the leaf one more time.
5. Color in your leaf outlines. Now color a red stripe down each side of the paper.

PEOPLE IN CANADA ARE PROUD OF THEIR FLAG

Index

Words to Know

Arctic—the frozen area around the North Pole

continent—one of Earth's seven big pieces of land

moss—a very short, leafy plant that grows in damp places

Native Americans—the first groups of people to ever live in North America

traded—gave one thing (such as guns) to get something else (such as food)

Read More

Haugen, Brenda. *Canada ABCs: A Book About the People and Places of Canada.* Minneapolis: Picture Window Books, 2004.

Orr, Tamra. *Canada.* New York: Children's Press, 2005.

Quigley, Mary. *Canada.* Chicago: Heinemann Library, 2003.

Explore the Web

A Bird's Eye View! http://collections.ic.gc.ca/eyeview

The Big Blue Bus—The Small Fry Club http://www.dfo-mpo.gc.ca/canwaters-eauxcan/bbb-lgb/fry-alevins/index_e.asp

Zoom School: Canada http://www.enchantedlearning.com/school/Canada